Beyond Faith

Living in God's Kingdom on Earth.

Heir of the Anointed

Dhr. Jerry Amoa Owusu Addai

CONTENTS

CHAPTER ONE

UNDERSTANDING THE KINGDOM OF GOD

Exploring the concept of the Kingdom of God

Understanding the Kingdom of God requires delving into a multifaceted concept that encompasses both theological and practical dimensions. At its core, the Kingdom of God represents God's sovereign rule over all creation, manifesting through both spiritual and physical realms. Unlike earthly kingdoms defined by geopolitical boundaries and human governance, God's kingdom is characterized by its divine nature, eternal existence, and foundational principles of righteousness, peace, and joy in the Holy Spirit.

The Kingdom of God is not merely a future promise but a present reality for believers, initiated by Jesus' ministry on Earth. Through parables and teachings, Jesus illustrated the kingdom's values, emphasizing love, justice, and humility over power and wealth. The kingdom is both already present, through the lives of those who follow Jesus, and not yet fully realized, awaiting its complete fulfillment when Jesus returns.

Understanding this kingdom involves recognizing it as the central theme of Jesus' ministry. He invited individuals to repent and believe the good news that the kingdom is near, offering a new way of life that contrasts sharply with the values of the world. This invitation extends to all, calling for a transformation of heart and mind that aligns with God's desires.

Living under the Kingdom of God means embracing a life governed by divine laws and principles, which are outlined in the Scriptures. These principles guide believers in their conduct, relationships with others, and engagement with society. The kingdom's citizens are encouraged to exhibit qualities such as love, mercy, and forgiveness, reflecting the character of God in their daily lives.

Furthermore, understanding the Kingdom of God involves recognizing its communal aspect. Believers are called to be part of a community that lives out kingdom values, working together to demonstrate God's love and justice in the world. This includes acts of service, stewardship of creation, and advocacy for the marginalized and oppressed, showcasing the kingdom's transformative power in tangible ways.

In summary, the Kingdom of God is a profound and comprehensive concept that transcends traditional notions of religion and spirituality. It calls for a holistic commitment to living according to God's will, marked by a deep-seated desire to see God's justice, peace, and righteousness flourish in every aspect of life. By understanding and embracing the principles of God's kingdom, believers are empowered to make a significant impact in the world, contributing to the ongoing realization of heaven on earth.

CHAPTER TWO

THE IMPORTANCE OF DIVINE GUIDANCE IN HUMAN LIFE

Discussing the basics of spiritual enlightenment and its role in understanding divine wisdom.

The importance of divine guidance in human life cannot be overstated, as it serves as a compass for moral and ethical decision-making, personal growth, and understanding one's purpose in the world. Divine guidance, rooted in religious and spiritual beliefs, offers a framework for living that transcends the materialistic and often chaotic nature of daily life. It provides individuals with a sense of direction, peace, and resilience in the face of adversity, grounding them in values that promote compassion, integrity, and the welfare of the community.

Engaging with divine guidance involves more than adherence to religious rituals; it entails an ongoing dialogue with the transcendent, seeking wisdom and insight for life's challenges. This guidance shapes not only personal choices but also influences the way one interacts with others, fostering a society that values justice, mercy, and mutual respect. By aligning one's actions with divine principles, individuals can contribute to a more harmonious and equitable world.

Moreover, divine guidance encourages introspection and self-improvement, urging individuals to reflect on their lives and aspire towards higher moral and spiritual standards. This introspective journey enhances one's character and relationships, leading to a more fulfilling and purpose-driven life. In essence, divine guidance is pivotal for navigating the complexities of human existence, offering a path to inner peace and societal harmony.

CHAPTER THREE

FOUNDATIONS OF THE KINGDOM

Historical Ignorance and Divine Wisdom

Historical ignorance significantly impacts our understanding of divine wisdom and our place within God's kingdom. This segment explores the critical role history plays in shaping our perceptions of spirituality and divine governance, highlighting the necessity of integrating historical awareness with divine guidance for a holistic understanding of our purpose and place in the universe.

History is not just a collection of dates and events but a rich tapestry that records the interaction between the divine and humanity. It offers insights into how divine principles have been understood, interpreted, and applied across different epochs. By studying history, we uncover how divine wisdom has guided societies, influenced leaders, and shaped civilizations. This understanding is crucial for recognizing patterns of divine intervention and governance, providing us with a roadmap for aligning our lives with the principles of God's kingdom.

Ignorance of this historical dimension leaves us at a disadvantage, akin to navigating a complex landscape without a map. It results in a fragmented understanding of our spirituality, where divine guidance is seen as abstract or irrelevant to daily life. Conversely, embracing our historical heritage as a part of God's continuous narrative allows us to see ourselves as participants in a divine kingdom that transcends time and space.

Divine wisdom, as revealed through history, teaches us about the nature of God's kingdom. It is not merely a spiritual realm but a comprehensive system of governance that encompasses every aspect of human existence. This wisdom instructs us on how to live in accordance with divine laws, embodying values such as justice, compassion, and righteousness in our personal and communal lives.

Moreover, historical awareness fosters a deeper appreciation for the Bible as a living document that has guided countless generations towards understanding their divine rights and responsibilities. It presents the Bible not just as a religious text but as a constitutional framework for living under the sovereignty of God. This perspective encourages us to engage with the Bible as active citizens of God's kingdom, seeking to understand and apply its principles in a contemporary context.

In conclusion, bridging the gap between historical ignorance and divine wisdom is essential for realizing our place in God's kingdom. By valuing our historical roots and the divine guidance that has shaped human civilization, we can better appreciate the relevance of divine laws in today's world. This approach not only enriches our spiritual lives but also empowers us to contribute to the manifestation of heaven on Earth, where divine principles guide human affairs. Through this synthesis of historical insight and divine wisdom, we are better equipped to navigate the challenges of the present, inspired by the lessons of the past and guided by the timeless governance of God's kingdom.

CHAPTER FOUR

DIVINE WISDOM AS A SOLUTION TO IGNORANCE

The chapter on "Historical Ignorance and Divine Wisdom" addresses the profound gap in human understanding that stems from a lack of awareness about our historical context and roots. This ignorance not only confines individuals to a repetitive cycle of mistakes but also hinders their ability to envision and manifest a future that aligns with divine intentions for humanity. The text argues that to break free from this cycle of ignorance, humanity must turn towards divine wisdom, which offers insights that transcend time and human limitations.

Divine wisdom, as presented in this context, is not merely about religious beliefs or practices; it is about accessing a higher level of understanding and guidance that has been provided through sacred texts and spiritual teachings. This wisdom offers solutions to the complex problems of modern life, providing principles for governance, social justice, personal conduct, and environmental stewardship that are sorely needed in today's world.

The concept of divine wisdom as a solution to ignorance is rooted in the belief that there is a divine plan for humanity, a plan that offers prosperity, peace, and fulfilment. However, accessing this wisdom requires humility, openness, and a willingness to learn and apply these higher principles in our lives. It challenges readers to consider the long-term consequences of their actions and decisions, urging them to align their lives with a greater good that benefits not just themselves but the entire human community.

This section emphasizes that divine wisdom is available to all who seek it, regardless of their background or faith tradition. It encourages individuals to delve into their spiritual heritage, to study and reflect upon the teachings that have guided civilizations for millennia. By doing so, individuals can begin to see beyond the immediate, beyond the material, and into the heart of what it means to be truly human in harmony with the divine.

Moreover, the chapter advocates for an educational system and societal norms that integrate divine wisdom into their core, suggesting that such an integration could lead to a more enlightened, just, and peaceful world. It calls for a reevaluation of current values and priorities, proposing that a society guided by divine wisdom would prioritize the well-being of all its citizens, the stewardship of the earth, and the pursuit of justice and equity.

"Historical Ignorance and Divine Wisdom" posits that the antidote to our collective ignorance lies in embracing and implementing the timeless wisdom that has been passed down through generations. It is a call to action for individuals and societies to recognize the limitations of a solely secular perspective and to open their hearts and minds to the transformative power of divine guidance. This shift, the chapter suggests, could lead us closer to realizing heaven on Earth, where human actions are in harmony with divine will, leading to a more fulfilling and sustainable existence for all.

CHAPTER FIVE

THE DIVINE CONSTITUTION: INTERPRETING THE BIBLE

The Bible as a constitutional document for life

"The Divine Constitution: Interpreting the Bible" delves into the profound significance of the Bible as more than just a religious text, but as a foundational document that offers principles for living a fulfilling and purposeful life. Much like a constitution provides the framework for a nation's governance, the Bible lays out guidelines for moral conduct, personal development, and societal harmony.

At its core, the Bible serves as a timeless guidebook, offering insights into the nature of God, the purpose of humanity, and the principles that govern human behaviour. It is viewed in this context as a "divine constitution," providing a framework for understanding our relationship with the divine and with one another.

The chapter explores various methods of interpreting the Bible, recognizing that its ancient texts are rich with symbolism, metaphor, and cultural context. It emphasizes the importance of approaching the Bible with humility and reverence, seeking to understand its deeper truths rather than simply extracting literal meanings. This interpretive approach allows readers to uncover layers of wisdom that transcend time and culture, making the Bible relevant and applicable to contemporary life.

Furthermore, the text underscores the dynamic nature of biblical interpretation, acknowledging that different individuals and communities may derive varying interpretations from the same passages. However, it emphasizes the importance of interpreting the Bible through the lens of love, justice, and compassion, guiding readers towards interpretations that promote harmony and goodwill.

The chapter also addresses the challenges and controversies surrounding biblical interpretation, acknowledging that interpretations have been used to justify everything from acts of love and compassion to acts of violence and oppression. It calls on readers to critically engage with the text, recognizing that interpretations must be grounded in an understanding of historical context, cultural background, and theological principles.

Moreover, the chapter highlights the transformative power of biblical interpretation, noting that when approached with an open heart and mind, the Bible can inspire profound personal growth and spiritual awakening. It encourages readers to delve deeply into the text, engaging in prayer, meditation, and study to unlock its hidden treasures.

Ultimately, "The Divine Constitution: Interpreting the Bible" invites readers to view the Bible not merely as a religious artifact, but as a living document that speaks to the deepest aspirations of the human spirit. It calls on individuals to embrace the wisdom contained within its pages, allowing it to guide their thoughts, words, and actions in ways that honour the divine and promote the common good. In doing so, readers can unlock the transformative power of the Bible and experience a deeper sense of purpose, meaning, and fulfilment in their lives.

THE DIVINE CONSTITUTION: INTERPRETING THE BIBLE

Principles for living under God's governance

Living under God's governance entails adhering to a set of principles derived from divine guidance as outlined in the Bible. These principles serve as a blueprint for navigating life under God's will and establishing a harmonious relationship with Him. Here are some fundamental principles for living under God's governance:

Obedience to Divine Laws

Central to living under God's governance is obedience to His laws. The Bible provides clear instructions on how to live a righteous and fulfilling life, and adhering to these laws demonstrates reverence for God's authority. By following His commandments, individuals align themselves with His divine will and experience the blessings that come from obedience.

Love and Compassion

Love and compassion are foundational principles in God's kingdom. Jesus emphasized the importance of loving God and loving others as oneself. Living under God's governance requires treating others with kindness, empathy, and compassion, mirroring God's unconditional love for humanity. By extending love and compassion to others, individuals reflect the character of God and contribute to building a more loving and harmonious society.

Humility and Submission

Humility and submission are key attitudes for living under God's governance. Recognizing one's own limitations and submitting to God's authority fosters a humble and teachable spirit. Humility allows individuals to acknowledge their dependence on God and trust in His wisdom and guidance. By surrendering control and submitting to God's will, individuals position themselves to experience His grace and favor.

Justice and Righteousness

Justice and righteousness are integral aspects of God's governance. God is just and righteous, and He calls His followers to uphold these principles in their interactions with others. Living justly involves treating all people with fairness, equality, and integrity, while righteousness entails living in accordance with God's moral standards. By seeking justice and righteousness, individuals contribute to the establishment of God's kingdom on Earth and reflect His character to the world.

Faith and Trust

Faith and trust are essential for living under God's governance. Trusting in God's faithfulness and provision enables individuals to navigate life's challenges with confidence and peace. Faith involves believing in God's promises and relying on His strength and guidance in all circumstances. By placing their trust in God, individuals demonstrate their dependence on Him and experience the transformative power of faith in their lives.

Stewardship and Generosity

Stewardship and generosity reflect the principle of recognizing God as the ultimate owner of all resources. Living under God's governance involves responsibly managing the resources entrusted to us and using them to bless others. Stewardship encompasses wise financial management, environmental stewardship, and the responsible use of talents and abilities. By practising generosity and stewardship, individuals honour God's provision and contribute to His kingdom work on Earth.

Living under God's governance requires adherence to these fundamental principles derived from divine guidance. Obedience to God's laws, love and compassion for others, humility and submission to God's authority, justice and righteousness in all dealings, faith and trust in God's faithfulness, and stewardship and generosity in resource management are essential for experiencing the blessings of God's kingdom and fulfilling His purposes in the world. By embracing these principles, individuals can live lives that reflect the values of God's kingdom and participate in His redemptive work on Earth.

CHAPTER SEVEN

THE SOVEREIGNTY OF GOD

Rejecting traditional views of God's role

In understanding the concept of the sovereignty of God, it is essential to challenge and, in some cases, reject traditional views that may limit or misrepresent the nature of God's role in the universe. Traditionally, God has been depicted primarily as a distant, authoritarian figure who intervenes in human affairs according to His own will, often perceived as arbitrary and unpredictable. However, this narrow understanding fails to capture the richness and complexity of God's sovereignty as depicted in the Bible and other religious texts.

First and foremost, it is crucial to recognize that God's sovereignty is not synonymous with arbitrary control. While God is indeed depicted as the ultimate authority in many religious traditions, this sovereignty is often portrayed in conjunction with qualities such as love, justice, and mercy. Rather than viewing God's sovereignty as a license for capricious actions, it is more accurate to understand it as the foundation for a just and orderly universe.

Moreover, traditional views of God's sovereignty often emphasize His transcendence to the exclusion of His immanence. In other words, God is seen as separate from and above His creation, intervening only sporadically and from a distance. However, this perspective overlooks the profound intimacy and involvement that many religious traditions ascribe to God. From the Christian concept of the incarnation to the Islamic belief in Allah's closeness to His creation, there are numerous examples of God's immanent presence in the world. Rejecting traditional views of God's sovereignty requires acknowledging and embracing this immanence as an essential aspect of His divine nature.

Furthermore, traditional views of God's sovereignty often fail to account for the complexities of human free will. If God is truly sovereign, the argument goes, then human beings must be mere puppets on His string, with no real ability to choose or act independently. However, this deterministic understanding overlooks the profound mystery of human freedom and agency. While God's sovereignty may indeed encompass all of creation, including human beings, it does not negate our capacity for choice and responsibility. Instead, it invites us to participate in the unfolding of God's divine plan through our actions and decisions.

In rejecting traditional views of God's sovereignty, it is essential to embrace a more nuanced and expansive understanding that honours the complexity of divine revelation. Rather than reducing God to a simplistic caricature of absolute control, we must recognize Him as the sovereign ruler of the universe whose authority is tempered by love, justice, and mercy. We must also acknowledge His immanent presence in the world and the profound mystery of human freedom. By doing so, we can move beyond narrow theological constructs and embrace a more profound and transformative vision of God's sovereignty.

Chapter Eight

Understanding God as a Sovereign King

In the vast tapestry of theological discourse, one of the most fundamental yet profound concepts is the understanding of God as a sovereign king. This perspective transcends the traditional view of God as a distant, ethereal being, and instead presents Him as an actively ruling monarch with absolute authority over all creation. To grasp the significance of this concept is to delve into the heart of divine governance and the nature of God's relationship with humanity.

At its core, the notion of God as a sovereign king acknowledges His supreme authority and power over the universe. Just as a monarch reigns over his kingdom, God reigns over all existence, from the majestic galaxies to the smallest subatomic particles. This sovereignty is not merely symbolic or ceremonial; it is an inherent aspect of God's nature, woven into the fabric of reality itself. In recognizing God's sovereignty, we affirm His omnipotence, omniscience, and omnipresence—attributes that set Him apart as the supreme ruler of all creation.

Moreover, the concept of God as a sovereign king carries profound implications for human existence. As subjects of God's kingdom, we are called to recognize His authority and submit ourselves to His rule. This entails obedience to His commands, adherence to His laws, and acknowledgement of His lordship over every aspect of our lives. Just as citizens are bound by the laws of their earthly sovereign, so too are we bound by the divine laws that govern God's kingdom.

Yet, far from being a tyrant or despot, God rules with wisdom, justice, and love. His sovereignty is not characterized by arbitrary whims or capricious decrees but by perfect righteousness and benevolence. His laws are not burdensome shackles that constrain our freedom, but guiding principles that lead us to true fulfillment and flourishing. In submitting to God's sovereignty, we find not bondage, but freedom; not oppression, but liberation.

Furthermore, the concept of God as a sovereign king provides a framework for understanding the unfolding of history and the divine purpose behind it. Just as earthly monarchs govern their realms according to a predetermined plan, so too does God govern the course of human history according to His sovereign will. Every event, every twist and turn of fate, is ultimately subject to His divine providence and serves His overarching purpose. Even in the face of adversity and chaos, we can take comfort in the knowledge that God's sovereign hand is at work, guiding and directing all things towards the fulfilment of His divine plan.

In conclusion, the understanding of God as a sovereign king is not merely a theological abstraction, but a profound truth that shapes our worldview and our relationship with the divine. It calls us to recognize God's absolute authority over all creation, to submit ourselves to His rule, and to trust in His wisdom and providence. In embracing God's sovereignty, we find not only a source of security and stability but also a profound sense of purpose and meaning amid life's uncertainties.

CHAPTER NINE

LIVING IN THE KINGDOM

Obedience to Divine Laws

Living in the kingdom of God entails a profound commitment to obedience to divine laws. Obedience is not merely a passive adherence to a set of rules; rather, it is an active engagement with the principles that govern God's kingdom. It is through obedience that individuals align their lives with the will of God and experience the fullness of His blessings.

At the heart of obedience to divine laws is the recognition of God's sovereignty. God, as the supreme ruler of the universe, has established laws that govern every aspect of life. These laws are not arbitrary dictates but are rooted in His character of love, justice, and righteousness. Therefore, obedience to divine laws is not a burden but a pathway to experiencing the abundant life that God desires for His people.

One of the central aspects of obedience to divine laws is adherence to the moral precepts outlined in the Bible. The Bible serves as a guidebook for righteous living, providing principles that govern relationships with God, oneself, and others. Obedience to these moral laws involves living a life characterized by love, compassion, honesty, and integrity. It requires individuals to prioritize God's will above their desires and to submit their lives to His authority.

Furthermore, obedience to divine laws extends beyond moral conduct to encompass all areas of life. This includes obedience to God's commands regarding stewardship, justice, and worship. Stewardship involves recognizing that all resources and talents are gifts from God and using them wisely for His glory. Justice entails standing up for the oppressed and marginalized, reflecting God's concern for the vulnerable in society. Worship involves acknowledging God's sovereignty and giving Him the honour and praise He deserves.

The call to obedience to divine laws is not always easy. It often requires sacrifice and self-denial, as individuals are called to relinquish their desires and preferences in favour of God's will. However, the rewards of obedience far outweigh the costs. Obedience leads to a deepening of intimacy with God, as individuals align themselves with His purposes and experience His presence in their lives. It also results in blessings and favour, as God honours those who honour Him with their obedience.

Moreover, obedience to divine laws is essential for the flourishing of God's kingdom on Earth. When individuals collectively obey God's commands, they contribute to the establishment of a society characterized by justice, righteousness, and peace. Conversely, disobedience leads to chaos, brokenness, and the deterioration of societal values.

In conclusion, obedience to divine laws is foundational to living in the kingdom of God. It involves aligning one's life with the principles outlined in the Bible and submitting to God's authority in every area of life. While obedience may require sacrifice and self-denial, it ultimately leads to intimacy with God, blessings, and the advancement of His kingdom on Earth. Therefore, let us strive to live lives characterized by obedience to divine laws, knowing that in doing so, we participate in God's redemptive work in the world.

CHAPTER TEN

THE SIGNIFICANCE OF OBEDIENCE IN THE KINGDOM

In the kingdom of God, obedience holds profound significance, serving as the cornerstone of a harmonious relationship between the sovereign and His subjects. Obedience goes beyond mere compliance with rules; it reflects a deep-seated reverence for divine authority and a willingness to align one's actions with God's will. This essay delves into the multifaceted importance of obedience within the kingdom, exploring its theological underpinnings, practical implications, and transformative power.

At its core, obedience in the kingdom stems from the recognition of God's sovereignty. As the supreme ruler, God's decrees and commandments carry inherent authority, demanding unwavering obedience from His subjects. Throughout scripture, obedience is portrayed as an essential aspect of faith and devotion, exemplified by the unwavering loyalty of figures like Abraham, Moses, and Jesus. Their obedience serves as a testament to the profound trust they placed in God's wisdom and guidance, regardless of the challenges or uncertainties they faced.

Moreover, obedience in the kingdom is not driven by fear or coercion but by love and reverence for God. It is an expression of gratitude for His boundless grace and a desire to honour His divine will. Jesus encapsulated this sentiment in His teachings, proclaiming, "If you love me, keep my commandments" (John 14:15). Obedience, therefore, becomes an act of love and devotion, deepening the spiritual connection between God and His followers.

Practically, obedience in the kingdom translates into a life lived according to divine principles and values. It entails submitting every aspect of one's life to God's authority, from personal morality and ethical conduct to relational dynamics and societal engagement. Through obedience, individuals demonstrate their commitment to righteousness and holiness, striving to embody the virtues espoused by Christ Himself.

Furthermore, obedience in the kingdom fosters a sense of unity and cohesion within the community of believers. By adhering to a common set of principles and guidelines, individuals contribute to the collective well-being and spiritual growth of the community. This shared commitment to obedience creates a supportive environment where accountability, encouragement, and mutual edification thrive.

However, the significance of obedience extends beyond individual and communal realms; it has profound implications for the fulfilment of God's purposes on Earth. Throughout scripture, obedience is intricately linked to blessings, favour, and divine intervention. The psalmist declares, "Blessed are all who fear the Lord, who walk in obedience to him" (Psalm 128:1). Obedience opens the floodgates of God's blessings, paving the way for His transformative work in the lives of individuals and nations.

Conversely, disobedience disrupts the harmony of the kingdom and invites consequences that hinder spiritual growth and flourishing.

The biblical narrative is replete with examples of the dire consequences of disobedience, from the fall of Adam and Eve to the exile of Israel. Disobedience fractures the relationship between God and His people, leading to spiritual stagnation, moral decay, and estrangement from divine favour.

In conclusion, obedience holds profound significance in the kingdom of God, reflecting a deep-seated reverence for divine authority and a commitment to aligning one's life with God's will. It is an act of love, gratitude, and devotion, driven by a desire to honour God and experience His blessings. Through obedience, individuals contribute to the unity, spiritual growth, and fulfilment of God's purposes on Earth, ushering in the transformative power of His kingdom.

CHAPTER ELEVEN

PRACTICAL WAYS TO LIVE BY DIVINE LAWS

Living by divine laws is not merely a theoretical concept but a practical way of life that shapes our daily actions and decisions. As followers of Jesus Christ, the King of all kings, we are called to adhere to His teachings and principles as outlined in the four Gospels of the Bible. These teachings serve as the foundation for living in alignment with the constitution of the kingdom of God.

Jesus Himself emphasized the importance of obeying divine laws and living according to His teachings. In the Gospel of Matthew, He instructs his followers, saying, "Therefore everyone who hears these words of mine and puts them into practice is like a wise man who built his house on the rock" (Matthew 7:24, NIV). This illustrates the significance of not only hearing but actively implementing Jesus's words in our lives.

Similarly, in the Gospel of John, Jesus declares, "If you love me, keep my commands" (John 14:15, NIV). This statement underscores the inseparable connection between love for Jesus and obedience to His teachings. By following His commands, we demonstrate our love for Him and align ourselves with the divine laws of His kingdom.

The Gospel of Luke records Jesus teaching his disciples about the principles of humility and servanthood, stating, "For even the Son of Man did not come to be served, but to serve, and to give his life as a ransom for many" (Luke 19:10, NIV). This highlights the importance of selflessness and sacrificial love in living out the values of God's kingdom.

Moreover, in the Gospel of Mark, Jesus emphasizes the need for repentance and belief in the gospel, proclaiming, "The time has come. The kingdom of God has come near. Repent and believe the good news!" (Mark 1:15, NIV). Repentance involves turning away from sin and embracing the transformative power of the gospel, aligning ourselves with the values and principles of God's kingdom.

As believers, we are called to view the Bible as the constitution of the kingdom of God, guiding our thoughts, actions, and decisions. The Apostle Paul writes to Timothy, "All Scripture is God-breathed and is useful for teaching, rebuking, correcting and training in righteousness, so that the servant of God may be thoroughly equipped for every good work" (2 Timothy 3:16-17, NIV). This underscores the authority and relevance of Scripture in shaping our lives according to divine laws.

Practical ways to live by divine laws include daily prayer and meditation on Scripture, seeking guidance and wisdom from God through His word. Additionally, cultivating a spirit of humility, love, and service towards others reflects the values of God's kingdom. Acts of kindness, forgiveness, and generosity demonstrate our commitment to living out the principles of Jesus's teachings.

In conclusion, living by divine laws involves actively applying the teachings of Jesus Christ in our daily lives, guided by the principles outlined in the Bible. By obeying His commands, demonstrating love for God and others, and aligning ourselves with the values of God's kingdom, we fulfil our calling as citizens of His eternal reign.

CHAPTER TWELVE

RIGHTS AND PRIVILEGES UNDER DIVINE KINGSHIP

Claiming our rights as citizens of God's kingdom

In the divine kingdom, each citizen possesses inherent rights and privileges granted by their sovereign ruler, God Himself. Jesus Christ, acknowledged as the King of all kings, provided profound insights into the nature of these rights and privileges throughout the four Gospels. His teachings serve as a cornerstone for understanding our role as citizens of God's kingdom and the privileges we are entitled to under His divine kingship. The Bible, revered as the constitution of the kingdom of God, serves as our guide in claiming and understanding these rights.

Jesus Christ emphasized the importance of recognizing and exercising our rights as citizens of God's kingdom. In the Gospel of Matthew, He delivered the Sermon on the Mount, a seminal discourse outlining the principles of kingdom living. Here, Jesus declared, "Blessed are the poor in spirit, for theirs is the kingdom of heaven" (Matthew 5:3). This proclamation highlights the divine privilege of belonging to God's kingdom, irrespective of worldly status or wealth. It underscores the inherent dignity and worth bestowed upon each citizen under their citizenship in the divine realm.

Moreover, Jesus expounded upon the concept of rights and privileges in His parables. In the parable of the prodigal son, recounted in the Gospel of Luke, Jesus depicted the unconditional love and forgiveness extended by the heavenly Father to His wayward child. Through this narrative, Jesus illustrates the divine privilege of reconciliation and restoration available to all who repent and return to God (Luke 15:11-32). As citizens of God's kingdom, we possess the right to experience the fullness of His grace and mercy, regardless of our past transgressions.

Furthermore, Jesus affirmed the rights of His followers to inherit eternal life and experience communion with God. In the Gospel of John, He declared, "I am the way, and the truth, and the life. No one comes to the Father except through me" (John 14:6). This statement encapsulates the fundamental privilege of intimate relationship with God, made possible through faith in Jesus Christ. As citizens of God's kingdom, we have the right to partake in the abundant life offered by our benevolent King and to experience eternal fellowship with Him.

The Bible serves as the authoritative constitution of the kingdom of God, delineating the rights and responsibilities of its citizens. In the epistles of Paul, the apostle elaborated on the privileges bestowed upon believers through their union with Christ. In his letter to the Ephesians, Paul affirmed, "But God, being rich in mercy, because of the great love with which he loved us, even when we were dead in our trespasses, made us alive together with Christ—by grace, you have been saved" (Ephesians 2:4-5). This passage underscores the divine privilege of salvation extended to all who believe in Jesus Christ, irrespective of their merit or worthiness.

In conclusion, as citizens of God's kingdom, we are endowed with inherent rights and privileges by our sovereign ruler, Jesus Christ. The teachings of Jesus and the Scriptures serve as our guide in claiming and understanding these privileges, which include reconciliation, eternal life, and communion with God. Let us, therefore, embrace our identity as citizens of the divine realm and live out the fullness of our rights and privileges as bestowed by our gracious King.

CHAPTER THIRTEEN

THE PRIVILEGES OF LIVING UNDER DIVINE SOVEREIGNTY

Living under divine sovereignty is a privilege that transcends earthly status and temporal power. It is a profound realization that as citizens of God's kingdom, we are partakers of His divine authority and beneficiaries of His eternal grace. This privilege is beautifully encapsulated in the teachings of Jesus Christ, the King of all kings, as recorded in the four Gospels of the Bible.

In Matthew 5:3-12, commonly known as the Beatitudes, Jesus outlines the privileges bestowed upon those who live according to the principles of God's kingdom. He declares, "Blessed are the poor in spirit, for theirs is the kingdom of heaven... Blessed are those who hunger and thirst for righteousness, for they will be filled" (Matthew 5:3, 6, NIV). Here, Jesus emphasizes that the kingdom of heaven belongs to those who recognize their spiritual poverty and earnestly seek righteousness. It's a privilege granted to those who align their lives with God's will.

Moreover, in Matthew 6:33, Jesus instructs His followers, "But seek first his kingdom and his righteousness, and all these things will be given to you as well" (NIV). This verse underscores the privilege of priority in seeking God's kingdom. By prioritizing the kingdom of God and living in alignment with His righteousness, believers receive not only spiritual blessings but also the provision of their earthly needs.

In the Gospel of Luke, Jesus further elucidates the privileges of living under divine sovereignty through the parables He shared. In Luke 12:32, Jesus reassures His disciples, "Do not be afraid, little flock, for your Father has been pleased to give you the kingdom" (NIV). Here, Jesus highlights the Father's pleasure in granting His kingdom to His faithful followers. It's a privilege marked by divine favor and benevolence.

Additionally, in the parable of the Talents (Matthew 25:14-30), Jesus illustrates the rewards of faithful stewardship in the kingdom of God. The master entrusts his servants with different amounts of talents, symbolizing the diverse gifts and responsibilities given to believers. Those who faithfully invest and multiply their talents are commended with the privilege of entering into the joy of their master.

Throughout the Gospels, Jesus consistently emphasizes the kingdom of God as the central focus of His teachings. He urges His followers to embrace the privileges of citizenship in God's kingdom by adhering to its principles of love, righteousness, and service. Furthermore, Jesus affirms the Bible as the constitution of the kingdom of God, declaring in Matthew 4:4, "Man shall not live on bread alone, but on every word that comes from the mouth of God" (NIV).

In conclusion, living under divine sovereignty is a privilege marked by spiritual abundance, divine provision, and eternal inheritance. As citizens of God's kingdom, we are called to embrace the teachings of Jesus Christ, the King of all kings, and to live according to the constitution of the kingdom—the Word of God. May we recognize and cherish the unparalleled privileges bestowed upon us as children of the Most High, and may we faithfully steward our lives for the glory of His kingdom.

CHAPTER FOURTEEN

THE ROLE OF JESUS AND THE PROPHETS

Differentiating between Jesus and other prophets

In understanding the concept of God's kingdom and our place within it, it's essential to differentiate between Jesus and other prophets. While many spiritual leaders throughout history have conveyed divine messages, Jesus Christ stands apart as the ultimate source of divine knowledge and guidance. This distinction is firmly rooted in the teachings found within the Bible, which serves as the constitution of God's kingdom.

Throughout the four Gospels—Matthew, Mark, Luke, and John—Jesus Christ is depicted as not just another prophet, but as the King of all kings, ushering in a new era of divine sovereignty. His words and actions exemplify the principles of God's kingdom and serve as the foundation upon which believers are called to build their lives.

One of the central aspects that differentiate Jesus from other prophets is his claim to be the Son of God. In John 14:6, Jesus declares, "I am the way and the truth and the life. No one comes to the Father except through me." This statement underscores Jesus' unique role as the mediator between humanity and God, emphasizing his divine nature and authority.

Furthermore, Jesus frequently spoke about the kingdom of God, describing its principles and inviting people to enter into its reality. In Mark 1:15, he proclaims, "The time has come," he said. "The kingdom of God has come near. Repent and believe the good news!" Here, Jesus announces the imminent arrival of God's kingdom and calls for repentance and faith as prerequisites for entering into it.

In contrast to other prophets who merely relayed messages from God, Jesus spoke with authority, as noted in Matthew 7:28-29: "When Jesus had finished saying these things, the crowds were amazed at his teaching, because he taught as one who had authority, and not as their teachers of the law." This authority stemmed from his divine identity and intimate relationship with God the Father.

Moreover, Jesus' teachings went beyond moral instruction; they addressed the very nature of God's kingdom and the heart transformation required to enter it. In Matthew 5:20, he says, "For I tell you that unless your righteousness surpasses that of the Pharisees and the teachers of the law, you will certainly not enter the kingdom of heaven." Here, Jesus challenges his listeners to move beyond superficial adherence to religious laws and embrace a righteousness rooted in genuine faith and love.

While other prophets played significant roles in preparing the way for God's kingdom, Jesus Christ stands as the culmination of God's redemptive plan. Hebrews 1:1-2 affirms this: "In the past, God spoke to our ancestors through the prophets at many times and in various ways, but in these last days he has spoken to us by his Son, whom he appointed heir of all things, and through whom also he made the universe." Jesus' incarnation represents the ultimate expression of

God's love and mercy towards humanity, offering salvation and eternal life to all who believe in him.

In conclusion, the distinction between Jesus and other prophets lies in his unique identity as the Son of God and the King of all kings. His teachings, as recorded in the four Gospels, serve as the cornerstone of God's kingdom, inviting believers to follow him wholeheartedly and participate in the fulfilment of God's divine purposes. As we embrace Jesus' teachings and acknowledge him as the ultimate authority in our lives, we align ourselves with the constitution of God's kingdom, experiencing the abundant life and eternal blessings that come from living under his reign.

CHAPTER FIFTEEN

JESUS AS THE ULTIMATE SOURCE OF DIVINE KNOWLEDGE

Jesus Christ, revered as the King of all kings, stands as the ultimate source of divine knowledge for those seeking to understand and embody the principles of God's kingdom on Earth. His teachings, as recorded in the four Gospels of the Bible, serve as a foundational guide for believers, illuminating the path to living in accordance with the divine will.

Throughout the Gospels, Jesus imparted timeless wisdom that continues to resonate with humanity today. In Matthew 4:4, Jesus declares, "Man shall not live by bread alone, but by every word that comes from the mouth of God." This profound statement emphasizes the importance of spiritual nourishment and the primacy of divine guidance in sustaining human life. Here, Jesus establishes the precedence of prioritizing God's word as the ultimate source of sustenance and guidance.

Furthermore, in Matthew 5:17, Jesus affirms the enduring significance of the Old Testament scriptures, stating, "Do not think that I have come to abolish the Law or the Prophets; I have not come to abolish them but to fulfil them." This assertion underscores the continuity between the Old Testament and Jesus' teachings, positioning the Bible as a cohesive narrative outlining God's plan for humanity. Jesus' role as the fulfilment of prophecy reinforces the notion that the Bible serves as the constitution of God's kingdom, providing a framework for righteous living under His divine sovereignty.

In Matthew 22:37-40, Jesus encapsulates the essence of God's commandments, declaring, "Love the Lord your God with all your heart and with all your soul and with all your mind. This is the first and greatest commandment. And the second is like it: Love your neighbour as yourself. All the Law and the Prophets hang on these two commandments." Here, Jesus distils the complexities of divine law into a simple yet profound mandate: to love God wholeheartedly and to extend that love to others. This directive serves as the cornerstone of Christian ethics, illustrating the foundational principles upon which the kingdom of God operates.

Additionally, in John 14:6, Jesus proclaims, "I am the way and the truth and the life. No one comes to the Father except through me." This assertion underscores Jesus' unique role as the mediator between humanity and God, highlighting the centrality of his teachings in facilitating communion with the divine. As the embodiment of truth and life, Jesus serves as the ultimate authority on matters of spiritual significance, guiding believers towards a deeper understanding of God's kingdom and their place within it.

Incorporating these teachings into one's life requires a diligent study and application of the scriptures, recognizing the Bible as the constitution of the kingdom of God. By aligning one's actions and beliefs with the principles espoused by Jesus Christ, individuals can cultivate a deeper relationship with God and fulfil their purpose as citizens of His eternal kingdom.

CHAPTER SIXTEEN

The Kingdom in Practice

Education and Governance: Embracing Divine Wisdom

In the divine kingdom, education and governance are intricately intertwined, guided by the eternal principles outlined in the Bible, which serves as the constitution of God's kingdom on Earth. Jesus Christ, the King of all kings, imparted invaluable teachings throughout the four Gospels, shedding light on the fundamental aspects of education and governance within the kingdom.

Jesus, in his teachings, emphasized the importance of seeking divine wisdom above worldly knowledge. In Matthew 4:4, he declared, "Man shall not live by bread alone, but by every word that comes from the mouth of God." This profound statement underscores the significance of incorporating biblical teachings into education, highlighting the spiritual nourishment derived from the Word of God.

Moreover, Jesus demonstrated a unique approach to governance, contrasting earthly systems of power and authority. In Mark 10:42-45, he rebuked the disciples' desire for positions of power, stating, "Whoever wants to become great among you must be your servant, and whoever wants to be first must be slave of all. For even the Son of Man did not come to be served, but to serve, and to give his life as a ransom for many." Here, Jesus exemplifies servant leadership, emphasizing humility, selflessness, and sacrificial love as the pillars of governance in the kingdom.

Incorporating teachings from the book of Isaiah further illuminates the divine principles underlying education and governance. Isaiah 33:22 proclaims, "For the Lord is our judge, the Lord is our lawgiver, the Lord is our king; it is he who will save us." This verse encapsulates the essence of God's sovereignty over all aspects of human life, including education and governance. By acknowledging God as the ultimate authority, individuals and leaders are called to align their actions with His divine will, fostering justice, righteousness, and compassion in society.

In the context of education, the Bible serves as the ultimate source of truth and wisdom, shaping the minds and hearts of individuals to discern right from wrong. Proverbs 9:10 declares, "The fear of the Lord is the beginning of wisdom, and knowledge of the Holy One is understanding." This foundational principle underscores the centrality of God's Word in guiding educational curricula and fostering moral character, critical thinking, and spiritual discernment among students.

Similarly, in governance, leaders are called to uphold biblical principles of justice, equity, and compassion. Micah 6:8 exhorts, "He has shown you, O mortal, what is good. And what does the Lord require of you? To act justly and to love mercy and to walk humbly with your God." This directive emphasizes the moral responsibilities of leaders to govern with integrity, fairness, and compassion, reflecting God's character in their actions and decisions.

Education and governance in the divine kingdom are anchored in the timeless truths of the Bible, with Jesus Christ as the ultimate model of servant leadership. By embracing divine wisdom and aligning with

God's sovereign will, individuals and leaders can cultivate flourishing communities marked by justice, righteousness, and compassion, ushering in the realization of God's kingdom on Earth.

CHAPTER SEVENTEEN

THE IMPORTANCE OF DIVINE KNOWLEDGE IN EDUCATION AND GOVERNANCE

In both education and governance, the importance of divine knowledge cannot be overstated. This knowledge, derived from biblical teachings and the wisdom of God, serves as the foundation upon which individuals and societies can build prosperous and just communities. Drawing from the words of Jesus Christ, as recorded in the four Gospels, and the prophetic insights found in the book of Isaiah, we gain valuable insights into the principles that should guide both our educational endeavours and our systems of governance.

Jesus Christ, revered as the King of all kings, delivered teachings that transcended mere religious doctrines; they offered profound wisdom applicable to every aspect of life, including education and governance. In Matthew 22:37-40, Jesus succinctly encapsulates the essence of divine knowledge: "Love the Lord your God with all your heart and with all your soul and with all your mind... Love your neighbour as yourself. All the Law and the Prophets hang on these two commandments." Here, Jesus emphasizes the primacy of love and compassion in all human interactions, principles that should form the cornerstone of both education and governance.

Moreover, Jesus' teachings on humility, servanthood, and the inherent worth of every individual provide crucial guidance for both educators and leaders. In Matthew 20:26-28, Jesus declares, "Whoever wants to become great among you must be your servant, and whoever wants to be first must be your slave— just as the Son of Man did not come to be served, but to serve, and to give his life as a ransom for many." This profound statement challenges conventional notions of power and authority, advocating for servant leadership characterized by selflessness and sacrifice.

Similarly, the book of Isaiah offers prophetic insights into the nature of God's kingdom and the principles that should govern it. Isaiah 33:22 declares, "For the Lord is our judge, the Lord is our lawgiver, the Lord is our king; it is he who will save us." Here, we see a clear delineation of God's roles as the ultimate authority, legislator, and sovereign ruler. This passage reinforces the idea that divine knowledge, as revealed through scripture, should serve as the guiding force behind all human endeavours, including education and governance.

Incorporating biblical teachings into education fosters moral and ethical development, instilling in students virtues such as integrity, compassion, and justice. By grounding educational curricula in the principles of love and service espoused by Jesus Christ, educators can cultivate a generation of empathetic and responsible citizens equipped to contribute positively to society.

Likewise, governance informed by divine wisdom prioritizes the well-being of all individuals, particularly the marginalized and vulnerable. Leaders who emulate Jesus' example of servant leadership are more likely to enact policies that promote equity, justice, and the common good.

The importance of divine knowledge in education and governance cannot be overstated. By incorporating the teachings of Jesus Christ and the insights of biblical prophets into both realms, we can create communities characterized by love, justice, and compassion, fulfilling the vision of God's kingdom on Earth. The Bible, serving as the constitution of the kingdom of God, provides a timeless and authoritative guide for building a society that reflects God's will and purposes.

EXAMPLES OF SUCCESSFUL KINGDOM-BASED GOVERNANCE

In exploring examples of successful kingdom-based governance, it's essential to draw upon the teachings of Jesus Christ, the King of all kings, as well as insights from the book of Isaiah, while anchoring our understanding in the Bible as the constitution of the Kingdom of God. Across the four Gospels, Jesus provides profound wisdom and guidance on how to establish and maintain governance rooted in divine principles.

One key aspect emphasized by Jesus is servant leadership. In Mark 10:42-45, Jesus teaches his disciples about servant leadership, stating, "Whoever wants to become great among you must be your servant, and whoever wants to be first must be slave of all. For even the Son of Man did not come to be served, but to serve, and to give his life as a ransom for many." This principle underscores the importance of humility, selflessness, and sacrificial service in governance.

Additionally, Jesus teaches about justice and compassion. In Matthew 25:31-46, commonly known as the Parable of the Sheep and the Goats, Jesus speaks about the final judgment, highlighting the importance of caring for the marginalized and vulnerable. He identifies acts of compassion, such as feeding the hungry, clothing the naked, and visiting the sick and imprisoned, as integral to the Kingdom's values. This emphasizes the role of governance in ensuring equitable distribution of resources and upholding the dignity of all individuals.

Furthermore, Jesus emphasizes the importance of love and reconciliation in governance. In Matthew 5:9, he says, "Blessed are the peacemakers, for they will be called children of God." This teaching underscores the need for leaders to actively pursue peace, reconciliation, and unity within society. The Kingdom of God operates on principles of love and forgiveness, fostering harmony and cooperation among individuals and communities.

Turning to the book of Isaiah, we find prophetic insights into the nature of God's Kingdom and the qualities of its governance. Isaiah 11:1-9 portrays the ideal ruler, often interpreted as a reference to the Messiah, who embodies characteristics such as wisdom, understanding, counsel, might, knowledge, and fear of the Lord. This passage envisions a governance system marked by righteousness, equity, and justice, where the vulnerable are protected, and harmony prevails among all creation.

Incorporating these biblical teachings into governance requires aligning policies and practices with the values of the Kingdom of God as outlined in the Bible. The Bible serves as the constitution of the Kingdom, providing timeless principles and guidelines for just and compassionate governance. Leaders must prioritize serving others, pursuing justice, practising love and reconciliation, and upholding the dignity and rights of every individual.

Successful kingdom-based governance, therefore, reflects the transformative power of divine wisdom and guidance in shaping societies where justice, compassion, and righteousness prevail. By adhering to the teachings of Jesus Christ and drawing inspiration from the prophetic vision of Isaiah, leaders can establish governance systems that reflect the values of the Kingdom of God and contribute to the flourishing of all people.

CHAPTER NINETEEN

CHALLENGES OF CONTEMPORARY RELIGIOUS LEADERSHIP

Critique of modern religious practices

In examining the challenges of contemporary religious leadership, it becomes imperative to critique modern religious practices through the lens of biblical teachings. The essence of religious leadership should be rooted in the wisdom and guidance provided within the pages of the Bible, particularly focusing on the words of Jesus Christ, hailed as the King of all kings, as recorded in the four Gospels, as well as insights from the book of Isaiah.

One of the primary criticisms that contemporary religious leadership faces is the deviation from the core teachings of Jesus Christ. Throughout the Gospels, Jesus emphasized the importance of love, compassion, and humility. However, in many instances, modern religious practices seem to prioritize rituals, doctrines, and dogmas over these fundamental principles. Instead of fostering genuine spiritual growth and connection with God, these practices can often lead to division, judgment, and exclusion within religious communities.

Jesus' teachings consistently emphasized the inclusivity of God's kingdom. He welcomed sinners, healed the sick, and dined with outcasts, demonstrating a radical love that transcended societal norms and religious boundaries. Yet, contemporary religious leadership often falls short of mirroring this inclusive attitude. Instead of reaching out to the marginalized and embracing diversity, some religious leaders may perpetuate discrimination, prejudice, and exclusivity, contradicting the very essence of Jesus' message.

Furthermore, Jesus frequently condemned hypocrisy and self-righteousness among religious leaders of his time. He warned against the dangers of prioritizing outward displays of piety over genuine inner transformation. However, in the present day, there are instances where religious leaders may prioritize power, wealth, and prestige over humility and service. This departure from Jesus' teachings not only undermines the credibility of religious institutions but also hinders their ability to effectively convey the message of the Gospel.

Incorporating insights from the book of Isaiah further illuminates the responsibilities of religious leadership. Isaiah prophesied about the establishment of God's kingdom, envisioning a society characterized by justice, righteousness, and peace. He called upon leaders to act with integrity, to advocate for the oppressed, and to pursue reconciliation and restoration. However, when contemporary religious leaders fail to uphold these principles, they contribute to the perpetuation of injustice and inequality, tarnishing the reputation of religious institutions.

Thus, the Bible serves as the constitution of the kingdom of God, providing a framework for ethical leadership and communal living. It challenges contemporary religious leaders to reevaluate their practices and align them with the teachings of Jesus Christ and the prophetic insights of Isaiah. By prioritizing love, compassion, humility, and justice, religious leadership can reclaim its transformative potential and truly embody the principles of God's kingdom. It is through a sincere commitment to biblical wisdom that contemporary religious leaders can navigate the challenges of their time and lead their communities towards a deeper understanding of faith and a more authentic expression of worship.

CHAPTER TWENTY

CRITIQUE OF MODERN RELIGIOUS PRACTICES

In contemporary society, the landscape of religious practices often falls short of the ideal outlined in the biblical texts. The teachings of Jesus Christ proclaimed as the King of all kings, offer profound insights into the nature of true faith and the expectations of those who claim to follow Him. Drawing from the four Gospels—Matthew, Mark, Luke, and John—as well as the prophetic writings of Isaiah, we find a rich repository of wisdom that serves as a yardstick for evaluating modern religious practices. Moreover, the Bible itself, particularly when viewed through the lens of Jesus's teachings, emerges as the constitution of the kingdom of God, providing the framework within which true faith should be lived out.

One of the primary criticisms of modern religious practices lies in their tendency to prioritize outward displays of piety over genuine transformation of the heart. Jesus Himself admonished the religious leaders of His time for their hypocrisy, condemning their focus on religious rituals while neglecting justice, mercy, and faithfulness (Matthew 23:23). In contrast to this legalistic approach, Jesus emphasized the importance of inner righteousness, teaching that true worship involves loving God with all one's heart, soul, and mind, and loving one's neighbour as oneself (Matthew 22:37-39).

Furthermore, Jesus warned against the danger of mere lip service to God, cautioning His followers against empty religious practices devoid of genuine devotion (Matthew 15:8-9). He urged them to worship in spirit and in truth, emphasizing the need for authenticity and sincerity in their relationship with God (John 4:23-24). This stands in stark contrast to the superficial religiosity often prevalent in modern times, where adherence to religious traditions may take precedence over a genuine pursuit of God's will.

The prophet Isaiah similarly denounced empty religious rituals divorced from righteous living, declaring that God desires obedience and justice rather than sacrifices and offerings (Isaiah 1:11-17). This theme echoes throughout the Bible, reinforcing the idea that true faith is evidenced not merely by outward observance, but by a life characterized by righteousness and compassion.

Moreover, the Bible consistently presents Jesus as the embodiment of God's kingdom and the ultimate authority on matters of faith and practice. As the King of all kings, His teachings serve as the cornerstone of the kingdom of God, guiding believers in how to live out their faith in alignment with God's will. Therefore, any religious practice that deviates from the principles outlined by Jesus in the Gospels risks falling short of the standard set by the kingdom of God.

In conclusion, a critique of modern religious practices reveals a need for a return to the foundational teachings of Jesus Christ and a renewed commitment to living out the principles of the kingdom of God as outlined in the Bible. Rather than focusing solely on outward observance, true faith requires an inward transformation of the heart, characterized by love, justice, and obedience to God's will. By aligning our lives with the teachings of Jesus and allowing the Bible to serve as our constitution, we can strive toward a more authentic expression of faith that honours God and reflects His kingdom on earth.

CHAPTER TWENTY-ONE

ENCOURAGING DIRECT ENGAGEMENT WITH DIVINE LAWS

In the pursuit of living in God's kingdom on Earth, it is essential to encourage direct engagement with divine laws. These laws, as revealed in the Bible, serve as the foundation upon which the kingdom is built and sustained. By incorporating biblical texts, particularly those spoken by Jesus Christ, the King of all kings, as recorded in the four Gospels, and drawing wisdom from the book of Isaiah, believers are guided towards a deeper understanding of God's will and His governance over His kingdom.

Jesus Christ, being the ultimate authority and embodiment of God's kingdom, imparted invaluable teachings throughout His ministry. In the Gospels of Matthew, Mark, Luke, and John, His words resonate as directives for righteous living and governance within the kingdom of God. For instance, in the Sermon on the Mount

(Matthew 5-7), Jesus articulated foundational principles of the kingdom, such as humility, mercy, and love for one's enemies. He emphasized the importance of seeking righteousness above all else and taught his disciples to pray for God's kingdom to come and His will to be done on Earth as it is in Heaven (Matthew 6:10).

Furthermore, Jesus often used parables to convey profound truths about the kingdom of God. In the parable of the Good Samaritan (Luke 10:25-37), He illustrated the command to love one's neighbour as oneself, transcending social and cultural barriers. Through these teachings, Jesus provided a clear blueprint for ethical conduct and interpersonal relationships within the kingdom.

In addition to the teachings of Jesus, the prophetic words of Isaiah offer insights into the nature and governance of God's kingdom. In Isaiah 9:6-7, a prophecy concerning the Messiah declares, "For to us a child is born, to us a son is given, and the government will be on his shoulders. And he will be called Wonderful Counselor, Mighty God, Everlasting Father, Prince of Peace. Of the greatness of his government and peace, there will be no end." This passage highlights the divine authority and eternal reign of the Messiah, affirming His kingship over the kingdom of God.

Moreover, Isaiah 2:2-4 foretells a future where the nations will stream to the mountain of the Lord to learn His ways and walk in His paths, symbolizing the universal rule and peace of God's kingdom. These prophetic visions serve as a reminder of God's sovereign plan to establish His kingdom on Earth and invite believers to align themselves with His purposes.

Ultimately, the Bible stands as the constitution of the kingdom of God, providing the guiding principles and laws by which believers are called to live. By immersing themselves in Scripture, engaging directly with divine laws, and heeding the teachings of Jesus Christ, believers can actively participate in the realization of God's kingdom on Earth, bringing about transformation and renewal in their lives and communities.

CHAPTER TWENTY-TWO

MANIFESTING HEAVEN ON EARTH

Practical Steps to Manifest the Kingdom in Personal and Communal Life

In our pursuit to manifest heaven on Earth, it is imperative to turn to the foundational text of the kingdom of God: the Bible. This sacred scripture serves as the constitution guiding our lives under the sovereignty of God. Jesus Christ, revered as the King of all kings, left us with profound teachings in the four Gospels, offering invaluable insights into how we can bring the kingdom of God to fruition in our daily lives. Additionally, the prophetic words of Isaiah provide further guidance on living according to God's divine plan. By incorporating these biblical texts into our journey, we can embark on practical steps to manifest heaven on Earth.

Jesus Christ, during His earthly ministry, emphasized the importance of love, compassion, and righteousness as fundamental principles of the kingdom of God. In the Gospel of Matthew, He delivered the Sermon on the Mount, outlining the Beatitudes as a blueprint for kingdom living. Blessed are the peacemakers, for they will be called children of God. Blessed are those who hunger and thirst for righteousness, for they will be filled. These teachings underscore the significance of embodying virtues that reflect the character of God in our interactions with others and our pursuit of justice.

Furthermore, Jesus urged His followers to seek first the kingdom of God and His righteousness, promising that all other things would be added unto them (Matthew 6:33). This admonition reminds us of the priority of aligning our lives with God's will and purpose, trusting that He will provide for our needs as we prioritize His kingdom.

In the Gospel of Mark, Jesus proclaimed the arrival of the kingdom of God, calling for repentance and belief in the good news (Mark 1:14-15). This message invites us to turn away from sin and embrace the transformative power of the gospel, thereby ushering in the reign of God in our hearts and communities.

Moreover, the words of Isaiah resonate with prophetic vision, offering glimpses of a future where righteousness and peace abound under the reign of the Messiah. Isaiah 2:4 speaks of a time when nations will no longer wage war, but instead, they will beat their swords into ploughshares and their spears into pruning hooks. This imagery evokes a profound longing for a world transformed by the principles of God's kingdom—a world where justice and harmony prevail.

As we endeavour to manifest heaven on Earth, let us heed the teachings of Jesus Christ and the prophetic words of Isaiah. Let us strive to love one another, pursue righteousness, and seek the kingdom of God above all else. By anchoring our lives in the timeless truths of the Bible, we can actively participate in the realization of God's kingdom in our personal lives and our communities. As citizens of the kingdom of God, may we embody its values and principles, becoming agents of transformation in a world yearning for the peace and righteousness of heaven.

CHAPTER TWENTY-THREE

PRACTICAL STEPS TO MANIFEST THE KINGDOM IN PERSONAL AND COMMUNAL LIFE

I n manifesting the kingdom of God in personal and communal life, it is imperative to incorporate practical steps rooted in biblical teachings. The words of Jesus Christ hailed as the King of all kings, serve as a guiding light in this endeavour. Drawing from the four Gospels—Matthew, Mark, Luke, and John—as well as the prophetic book of Isaiah, and recognizing the Bible as the constitution of the kingdom of God, we find profound wisdom and guidance for transforming our lives and communities.

Jesus emphasized the importance of love, compassion, and service as foundational principles of the kingdom. In Matthew 22:37-39, he declared, "Love the Lord your God with all your heart and with all your soul and with all your mind... Love your neighbour as yourself." This commandment encapsulates the essence of kingdom living—loving God wholeheartedly and extending that love to others. Therefore, a practical step in manifesting the kingdom is to cultivate a heart of love towards God and neighbour, seeking ways to serve and uplift those around us.

Furthermore, Jesus emphasized the transformative power of forgiveness. In Matthew 6:14-15, he taught, "For if you forgive other people when they sin against you, your heavenly Father will also forgive you. But if you do not forgive others their sins, your Father will not forgive your sins." Forgiveness is a cornerstone of kingdom living, releasing us from bitterness and resentment and fostering reconciliation and healing in relationships. Practically, this entails extending forgiveness to those who have wronged us and seeking reconciliation where possible, thereby creating an atmosphere of peace and unity in our communities.

Moreover, Jesus highlighted the importance of humility and servanthood. In Mark 10:45, he proclaimed, "For even the Son of Man did not come to be served, but to serve, and to give his life as a ransom for many." Following his example, practical steps to manifest the kingdom include humbly serving others, putting their needs above our own, and using our gifts and resources to uplift the marginalized and oppressed in society.

Additionally, the prophet Isaiah foretold of a kingdom characterized by justice and righteousness. In Isaiah 1:17, he urged, "Learn to do right; seek justice. Defend the oppressed. Take up the cause of the fatherless; plead the case of the widow." Thus, practical steps in manifesting the kingdom involve actively advocating for justice and righteousness in our communities, standing up against oppression and injustice, and working towards systemic change that reflects God's heart for the marginalized and vulnerable.

In conclusion, manifesting the kingdom of God in personal and communal life requires aligning our actions with the teachings of Jesus Christ and the prophetic vision of Isaiah. By embodying love, forgiveness, humility, servanthood, justice, and righteousness, we can create a tangible expression of God's kingdom here on earth. Let us, therefore, commit ourselves to living out these principles daily, empowered by the transformative grace and power of God's spirit, and see the kingdom come in our midst.

CHAPTER TWENTY-FOUR

STORIES OF TRANSFORMATION AND RENEWAL

In the journey of embracing the kingdom of God on Earth, stories of transformation and renewal serve as powerful testimonies to the reality of divine guidance and the profound impact it can have on individual lives and communities. Drawing from the rich narratives found in the four Gospels, which serve as the foundational texts of the Christian faith and the constitution of the kingdom of God, we encounter numerous instances where Jesus Christ, the King of all kings, imparts timeless wisdom that continues to inspire and transform lives today.

One such story of transformation is that of Zacchaeus, a tax collector despised by his community for his corrupt practices. Despite his wealth, Zacchaeus felt a void within him until he encountered Jesus. Moved by Jesus' message of love and forgiveness, Zacchaeus repented of his sins and pledged to make amends by restoring fourfold to those he had wronged. This remarkable transformation not only impacted Zacchaeus personally but also brought about reconciliation and restoration within his community, demonstrating the transformative power of divine grace and the principles of the kingdom of God.

Similarly, the story of the woman caught in adultery offers a profound illustration of Jesus' compassion and mercy. When confronted by the religious leaders who sought to condemn her, Jesus responded with a challenge to those without sin to cast the first stone. As her accusers dispersed, Jesus extended forgiveness to the woman, urging her to go and sin no more. This encounter not only granted the woman a second chance but also revealed Jesus' role as the ultimate source of redemption and renewal, inviting all to experience the transformative power of his grace.

Furthermore, the parable of the prodigal son encapsulates the essence of renewal and reconciliation. In this parable, a wayward son squanders his inheritance in reckless living but ultimately returns to his father in humility and repentance. Rather than condemning him, the father embraces his son with open arms, celebrating his return with lavish grace and forgiveness. This story illustrates the boundless mercy of God and the invitation to all who have strayed to return to him and experience the joy of restoration and renewal.

These stories, among countless others found in the Gospels, serve as timeless reminders of the transformative power of divine love and grace. They invite us to embrace the principles of the kingdom of God as outlined in the Bible, recognizing Jesus Christ as the ultimate authority and guide in our lives. As we immerse ourselves in the teachings of Jesus and allow his words to shape our thoughts and actions, we open ourselves to the possibility of experiencing personal transformation and contributing to the renewal of our communities and the world at large.

Stories of transformation and renewal found in the Gospels offer profound insights into the nature of the kingdom of God and the transformative power of divine grace. By incorporating these biblical narratives into our lives and embracing Jesus Christ as the King of all kings, we can experience personal renewal and become agents of transformation in the world around us. As we strive to live according to the principles of the kingdom outlined in the Bible, we participate in the ongoing work of ushering in God's reign of justice, mercy, and love on Earth.

CHAPTER TWENTY-FIVE

CONCLUSION

The Call to Kingdom Living

As we reach the culmination of our exploration into living in God's kingdom on Earth, it is crucial to emphasize the profound significance of embracing this divine calling. Throughout this journey, we have delved into the foundational principles of the kingdom, examined the practical applications of divine wisdom in everyday life, and contemplated the transformative power of living according to God's sovereign rule. Now, as we conclude, let us heed the resounding call to fully embrace kingdom living in all its facets.

First and foremost, embracing kingdom living entails a radical shift in perspective. It requires us to recognize that our existence is intricately intertwined with the divine purpose and plan. No longer can we view ourselves as autonomous beings navigating the world in isolation. Instead, we must acknowledge our citizenship in God's kingdom and orient our lives accordingly. This shift in perspective empowers us to see beyond the temporal and embrace the eternal significance of our actions and decisions.

Furthermore, kingdom living compels us to prioritize obedience to divine laws above all else. In a world marked by moral relativism and ethical ambiguity, the steadfast adherence to God's commandments serves as a beacon of light guiding our path. It is through obedience that we align ourselves with the divine will and experience the fullness of God's blessings in our lives. As citizens of the kingdom, we are called to exemplify righteousness and integrity in all areas of our lives, serving as ambassadors of God's kingdom here on Earth.

Moreover, embracing kingdom living necessitates a rejection of the status quo and a commitment to transformative action. We cannot passively accept the injustices and inequities that plague our world; rather, we are called to actively work towards the realization of God's kingdom on Earth. This entails challenging systems of oppression, advocating for the marginalized, and promoting justice and equality in all spheres of society. It is through our collective efforts that we can begin to dismantle the barriers that hinder the manifestation of God's kingdom and usher in a new era of peace and harmony.

Additionally, kingdom living is characterized by a profound sense of hope and expectation. Even in the face of adversity and uncertainty, we hold fast to the promise of God's kingdom, knowing that His sovereign reign transcends all earthly limitations. This hope serves as an anchor for our souls, sustaining us through life's trials and tribulations and inspiring us to press onward in faith.

In conclusion, the call to kingdom living is not merely an abstract theological concept but a transformative reality that permeates every aspect of our lives. It beckons us to embrace a new way of being, characterized by obedience, justice, and hope. As we respond to this call, may we be ever mindful of our role as ambassadors of God's kingdom, tirelessly working to manifest His reign here on Earth. And may our lives serve as a testament to the transformative power of kingdom living, inspiring others to join us on this journey towards a brighter, more just future.

CHAPTER TWENTY-SIX

THE JOURNEY TO LIVING IN GOD'S KINGDOM ON EARTH

Living in God's kingdom on Earth is not just a distant aspiration; it's a journey that each individual can embark on right now. It begins with a fundamental shift in perspective, understanding, and commitment to living according to divine principles. This journey is not merely about religious observance or blind faith; it's about actively applying divine wisdom in everyday life to create a tangible experience of heaven on Earth.

At the core of this journey is the recognition of the Kingdom of God as a present reality rather than a distant future. It involves acknowledging God's sovereignty over all aspects of life and aligning one's thoughts, actions, and values with His divine will. This shift in perspective transforms how individuals approach challenges, make decisions, and interact with others.

The journey to living in God's kingdom on Earth begins with self-awareness and humility. It requires individuals to confront their own shortcomings, biases, and limitations, and to surrender their egos to divine guidance. This humility opens the door to receive divine wisdom and direction, enabling individuals to navigate life's complexities with clarity and purpose.

Central to this journey is the recognition of the Bible as more than just a religious text but as a blueprint for living under God's governance. The Bible provides timeless principles and teachings that serve as a compass for navigating the complexities of life. By studying and internalizing these teachings, individuals gain insight into God's character, His plans for humanity, and the values that define His kingdom.

Living in God's kingdom on Earth also entails obedience to divine laws. This obedience is not driven by fear or obligation but by a deep reverence for God and a desire to align one's life with His purposes. It involves making choices that honor God's commandments and prioritize His will above personal desires or societal norms.

Another crucial aspect of this journey is the recognition of one's rights and privileges as citizens of God's kingdom. This includes claiming the promises and blessings that God has bestowed upon His people, such as peace, joy, and abundant life. By embracing these rights and privileges, individuals experience the fullness of life that God intends for them.

Living in God's kingdom on Earth also requires active engagement with the world around us. It involves being agents of change and transformation, working to bring about God's kingdom values of justice, compassion, and reconciliation in every sphere of society. This may involve advocating for the marginalized, caring for the needy, and standing up against injustice and oppression.

Ultimately, the journey to living in God's kingdom on Earth is a lifelong process of growth, transformation, and discovery. It requires dedication, perseverance, and a willingness to continually seek God's guidance and direction. As individuals commit themselves to this journey, they experience the transformative power of divine wisdom, the joy of living in alignment with God's will, and the fulfillment of being part of something greater than themselves.

CHAPTER TWENTY-SEVEN

A Final Call to Embrace Divine Guidance and Righteousness

As we journey through the pages of this book, exploring the depths of God's kingdom and its implications for our lives, we inevitably reach a pivotal moment—a final call to action. It is a call not merely to understand or acknowledge, but to embrace wholeheartedly the divine guidance and righteousness that beckons us to live in alignment with God's will.

At the core of this call lies the recognition of our intrinsic connection to the divine. We are not mere bystanders in the unfolding drama of existence; rather, we are integral participants, endowed with the capacity to embody divine principles in our thoughts, words, and actions. It is through this embodiment that we truly manifest the kingdom of God on Earth.

Embracing divine guidance requires a profound shift in perspective—one that transcends the limited constructs of human understanding and surrenders to the wisdom of the divine. It beckons us to relinquish the illusion of control and trust in the inherent goodness and purpose of God's plan. In doing so, we open ourselves to a higher level of consciousness, one guided by love, compassion, and divine wisdom.

Central to this call is the imperative of righteousness—a commitment to living in accordance with divine laws and principles. Righteousness is not merely a moral code imposed from without, but a state of being that emanates from within—a reflection of our alignment with the divine essence that resides at the core of our being. It is through the cultivation of righteousness that we become vessels through which the divine can work its transformative power in the world.

To embrace divine guidance and righteousness is to embark on a journey of self-discovery and spiritual awakening—a journey that requires courage, humility, and unwavering faith. It is a journey fraught with challenges and obstacles, yet imbued with the promise of boundless grace and blessings.

In embracing divine guidance, we are called to surrender our egos and align our will with the divine will—to heed the whispers of the Spirit that guide us along the path of righteousness. It is a call to cultivate a deep and abiding relationship with the divine—to seek communion with the source of all truth, goodness, and beauty.

As we heed this final call, let us remember that we do not walk this path alone. We are accompanied by a host of divine messengers—angels, prophets, and saints—who stand as beacons of light, illuminating the way forward. And ultimately, we are held in the embrace of a loving and merciful God, who calls us each by name and invites us to dwell in the fullness of divine love for all eternity.

In closing, let us heed this final call with hearts open and spirits receptive, ready to embark on the journey of a lifetime—a journey that leads not only to the fulfilment of our destinies but to the realization of God's kingdom on Earth. May we walk this path with courage, conviction, and unwavering faith, knowing that we are guided, supported, and loved beyond measure.